MUSIC

A Pictorial Archive of Woodcuts & Engravings

841 Copyright-free Illustrations
for Artists & Designers
Selected by

JIM HARTER

Dover Publications, Inc.
New York

PUBLISHER'S NOTE

Graphic designers today are rediscovering the beauty and technical advantages offered by traditional woodcut and wood-engraved artwork. This medium of reproduction, brought to perfection over several centuries, reached its peak in the nineteenth, only to be largely superseded by halftone reproduction of photographs in the twentieth. Advertisers, collagists and all kinds of designers—now that this engraved picture material is no longer produced and is becoming extremely hard to find—recognize once more how adaptable it is to a wide variety of projects, and how well it complements typography.

Jim Harter, a well-known collagist and a practicing designer who knows what his colleagues want, has chosen the over 800 pictures in this volume from a vast array of rare magazines and catalogues, both American and European. The material he has selected reflects both the diversity of the subject and the variety of styles of which woodcut and wood-engraving were capable: from simple, bold line renderings to those so carefully worked that they achieve an almost impressionistic gradation of tone.

The illustrations include a large number of individual musical instruments from America, Europe and other cultures and from many periods from antiquity to the present (these isolated instruments are identified in captions wherever possible); an equally large number of instruments being played—held in the proper position by appropriately attired performers in typical situations; many scenes of singing (popular, folk, informal, operatic, concert, liturgical); portraits of great composers whose personalities symbolize the art of music (Mozart, Beethoven, Wagner, . . .; the composers are identified in captions); pictures of early record-playing equipment; silhouettes, vignettes and spots in many styles and moods; ornamental frames and cartouches with musical subjects; and decorative old-fashioned musical notation.

Music: A Pictorial Archive of Woodcuts and Engravings is a new work, first published by Dover Publications, Inc., in 1980.

DOVER *Pictorial Archive* SERIES

International Standard Book Number: 0-486-24002-9
Library of Congress Catalog Card Number: 80-67477

Manufactured in the United States of America
Dover Publications, Inc.
31 East 2nd Street
Mineola, N.Y. 11501

1: Violoncello. **2**: Viola. **3**: Violin. **4**: Double bass.

1

1: Violin.

2

3

1 & 2: Violins.

4

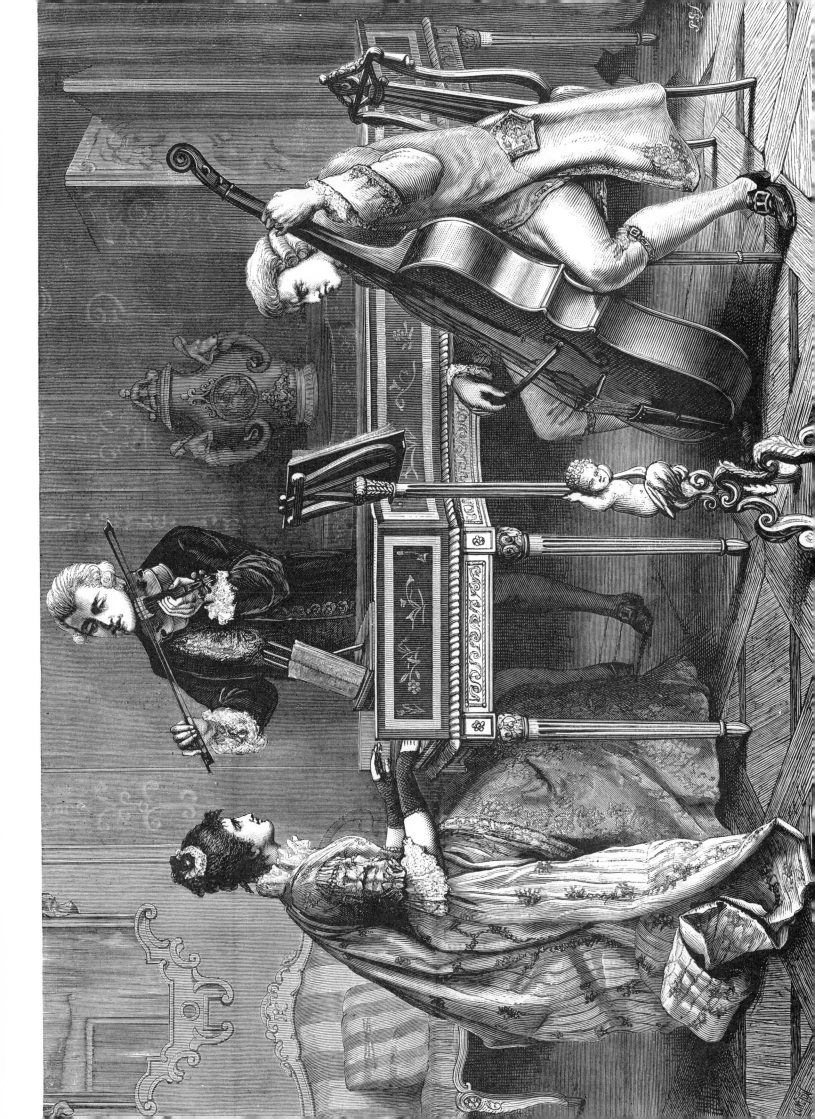

1: Twelve-stringed guitar. **2**: Nine-stringed Hawaiian guitar. **3**: Flat-backed mandolin. **4**: Royal mandolin.

1: Ukulele. 2: Twelve-stringed bass guitar. 3 & 4: Guitars.

1 & 2: Mandolins.

9

1: Banjo-mandolin. **2–5**: Banjos. **6**: Guitar-harp.

1: Natural horn.

1: Valve horn (French horn). 2: Keyed trumpet. 3: Sousaphone. 4: Bass tuba. 5: Cornet.

13

1: Trumpet. 2: Natural trumpet. 3: Bugle. 4: Slide trombone. 5: Valve trombone.

15

16   1: Posthorn. 2: Tuba. 3: Serpent. 4: Saxophone. 5 & 6: Bass clarinets. 7: Basset horn. 8: Bass tuba.

1: Contrabassoon. 2: Serpent. 3: Ophicleide. 4: Bass sarrusophone. 5-7: Basset horns. 8: Alto saxophone.

17

1: Buccina. **2**: Natural trumpet.

1: Hurdygurdy. **2**: Fagott.

24   1–3, 7, 8: Bassoons. 4: Oboe. 5: Oboe d'amore. 6: Oboe da caccia.

1–7, 10: Clarinets. 8: Bass clarinet. 9 & 11: English horns.

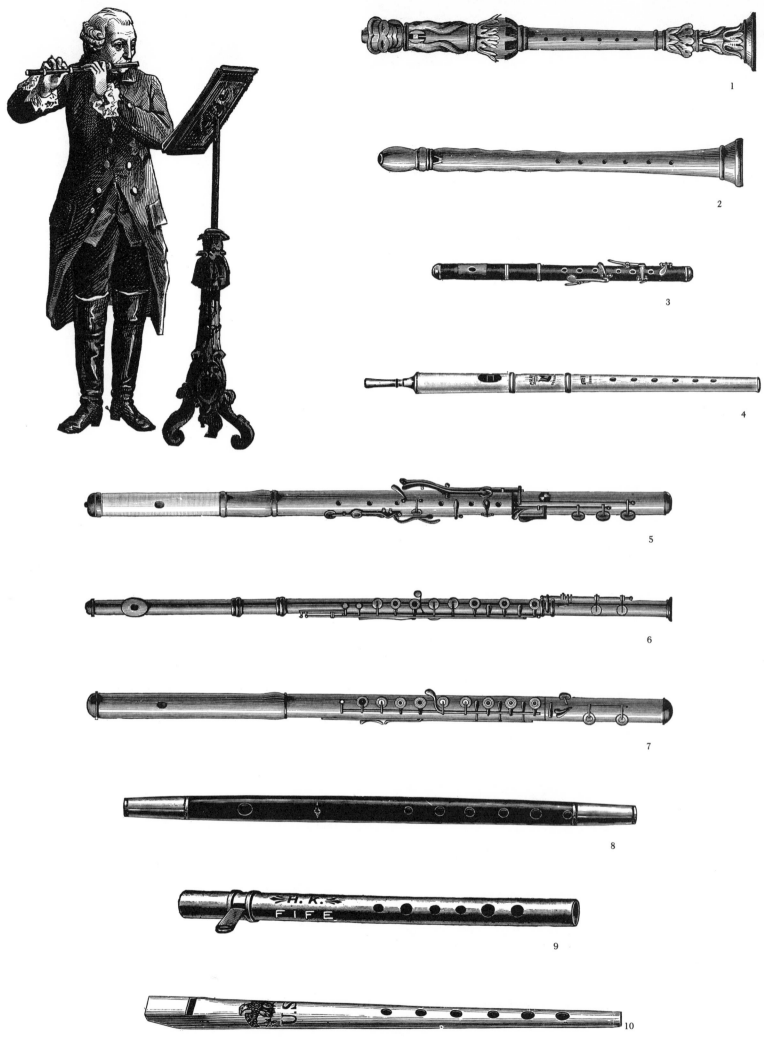

1

2

3

4

5

6

7

8

9

10

28   **1 & 2:** Recorders. **3:** Piccolo. **4 & 10:** Flageolets. **5–7:** Flutes. **8 & 9:** Fifes.

1: Flageolet. **2 & 6**: Flutes. **3 & 5**: Piccolos. **4**: Fife. **7**: Clarinet.

29

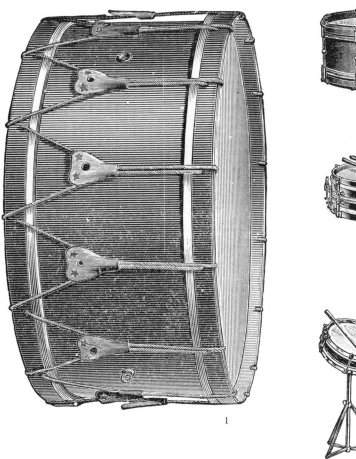

1: Bass drum. 2: Military drum. 3: Snare drum. 4: Collegiate drum set. 5: Professional trap drummer's set. 6: Prussian-style drum. 7: Kettledrum. 8: Side drum.

33

34

1 & 4: Cymbals. **2 & 5**: Castanets. **3**: Triangle.

Giuseppe Verdi conducting one of his own operas.

1: Concert zither. 2: Harp. 3: Zither. 4: Autoharp.

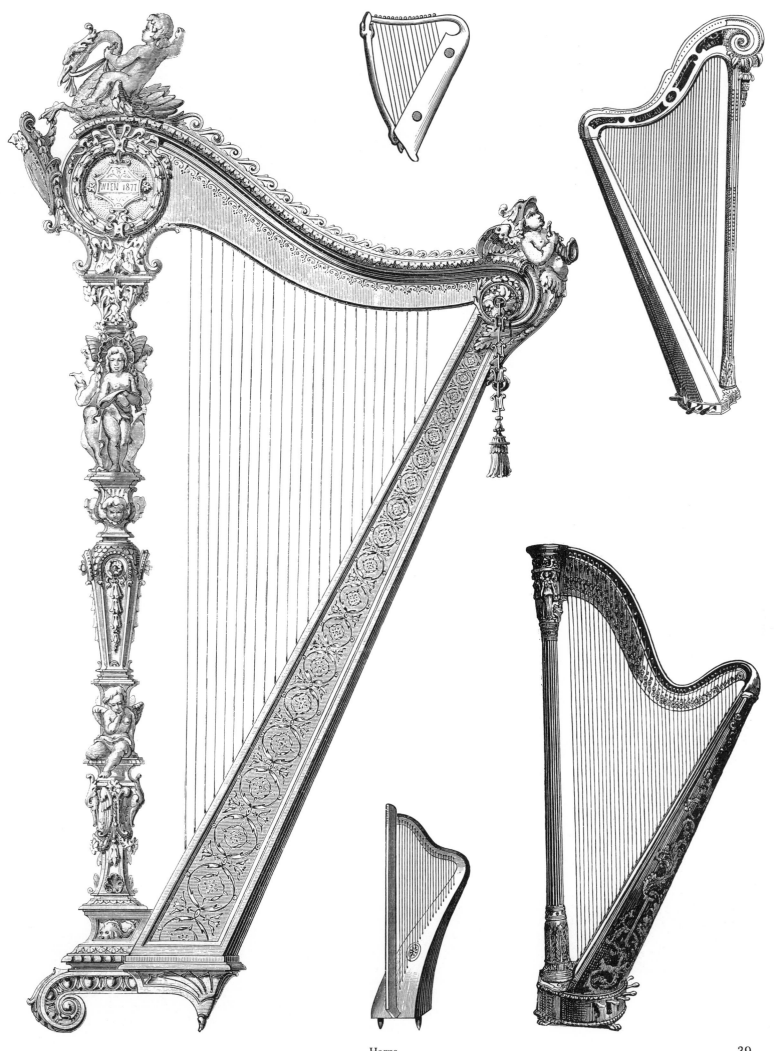

Harps.

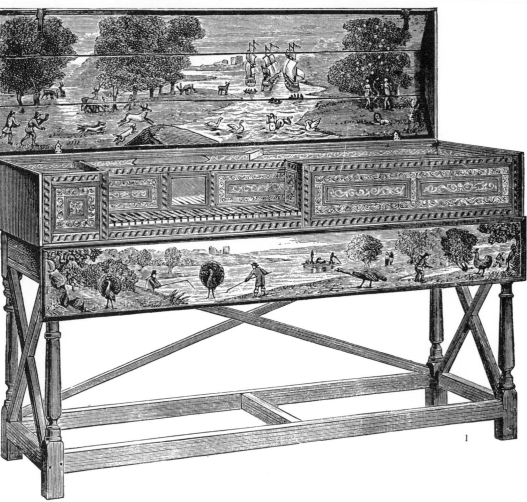

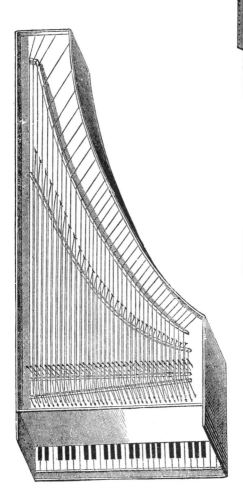

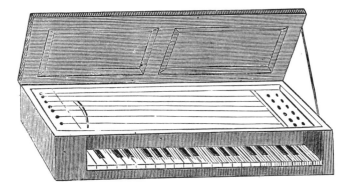

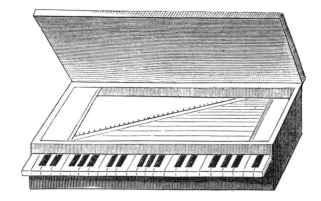

40

1 & 2: Pianos. 3: Spinet.

45

1 & 2: Pianos. **3**: Harmonium. **4**: Wolfgang Amadeus Mozart and his family. *Facing page*: Johann Sebastian Bach and his family.

Pianos.

1: Codonophone (a type of chimes). (All the rest are organs.)

49

Organs.

1: Pyrophone. 2: Gong. 3: Steam organ.

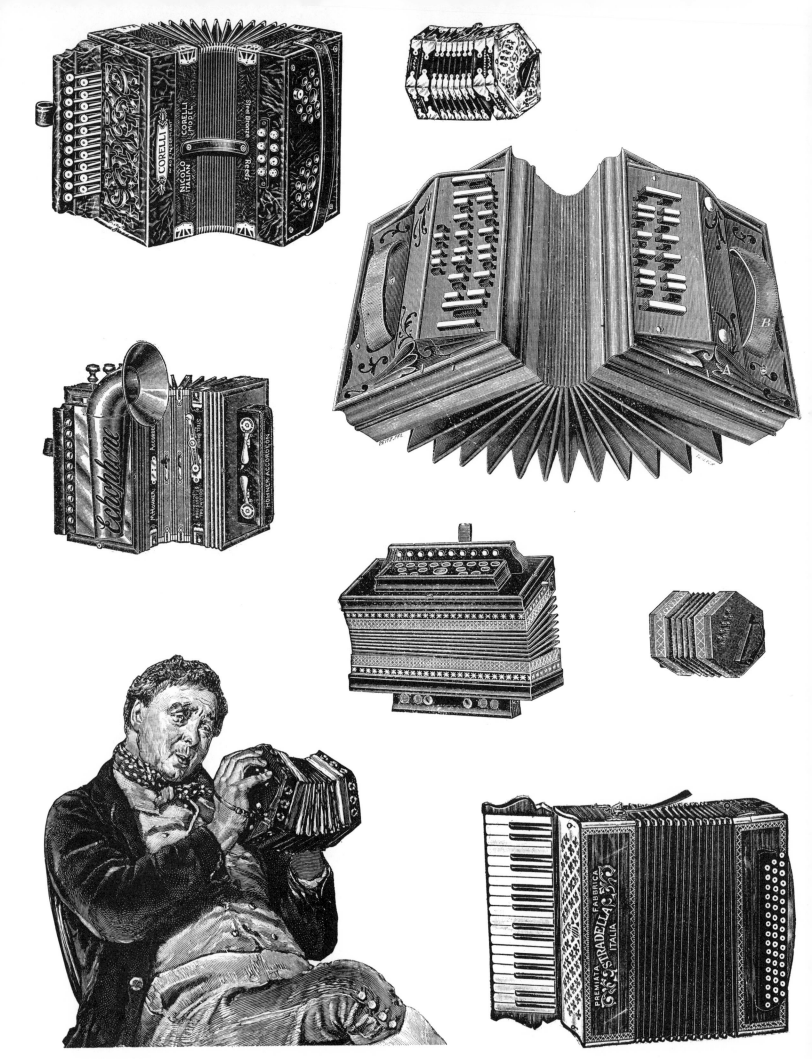

Accordions and concertinas.

53

1 & 2: Xylophones. 3 & 4: Orchestra bells. 5: Glockenspiel. 6: Metallophone.

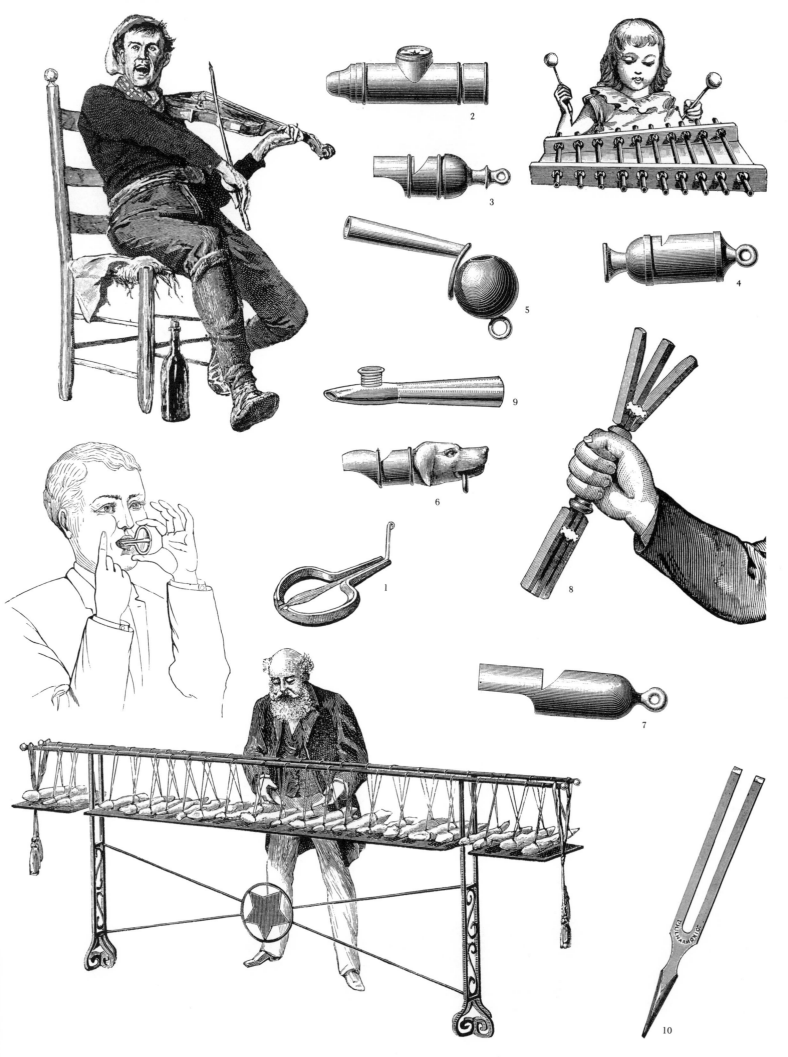

1: Jew's-harp. 2–7: Whistles. 8: Bones. 9: Kazoo. 10: Tuning fork.

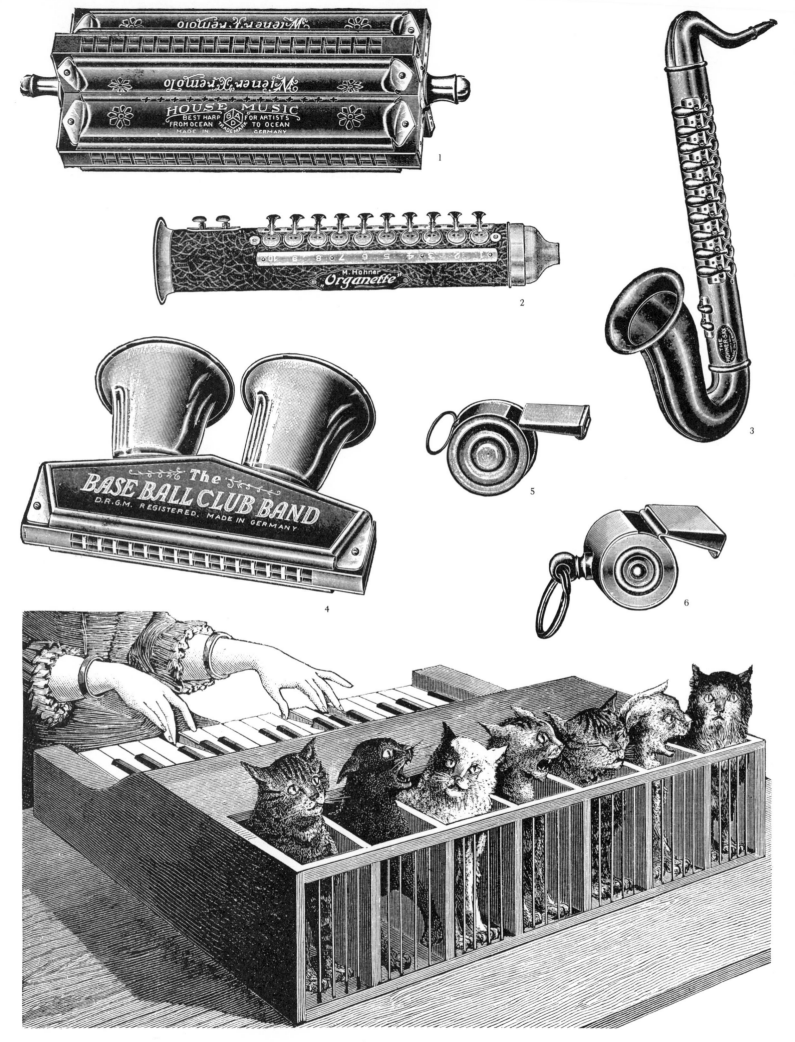

58   **1 & 4:** Harmonicas. **2:** Organette. **3:** Hohner-Sax. **5 & 6:** Whistles.

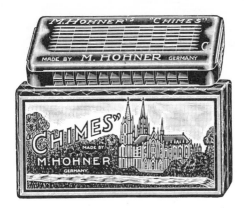

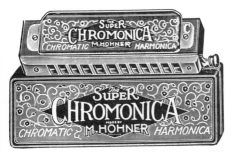

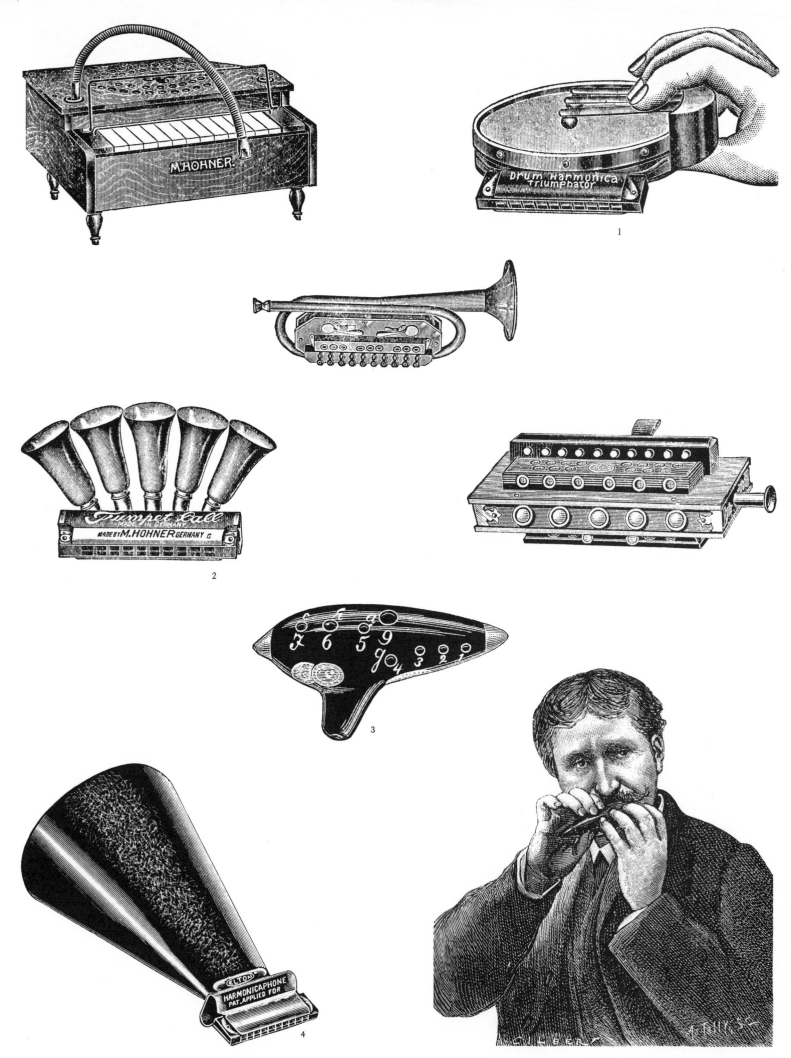

1: Drum harmonica. 2: Harmonica. 3: Ocarina. 4: Harmonicaphone.

1 & 2: Tambourines.

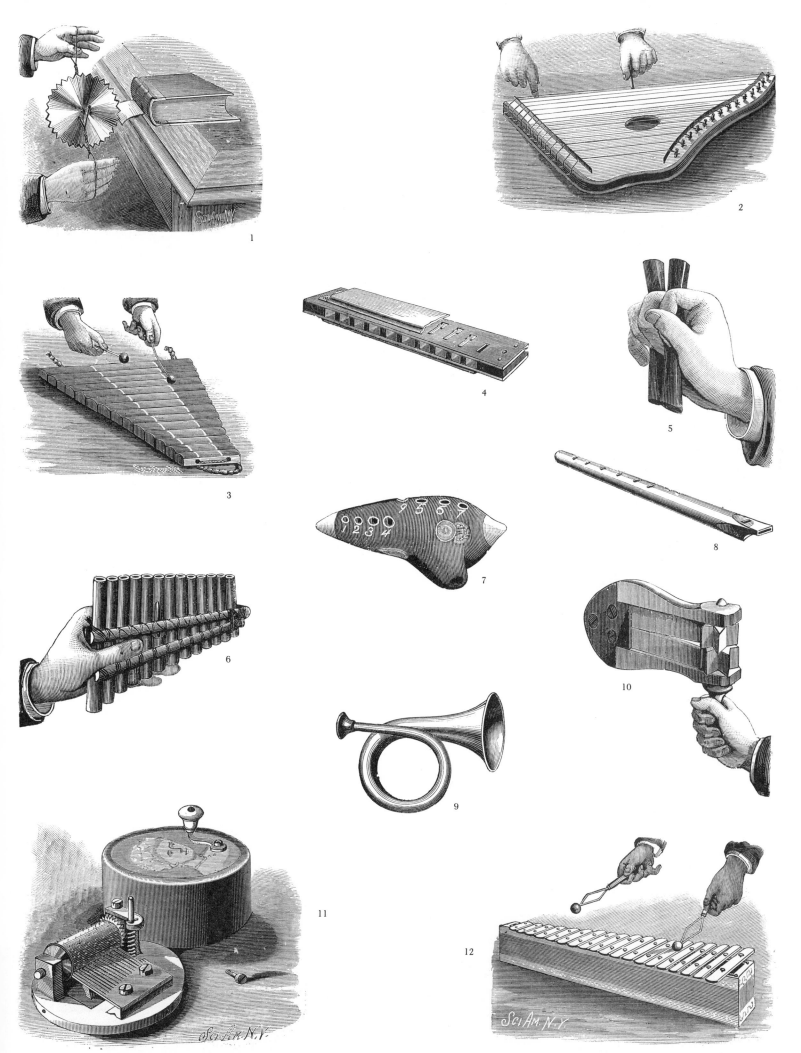

1: Buzz. 2: Zither. 3: Xylophone. 4: Harmonica. 5: Clappers. 6: Panpipes. 7: Ocarina. 8: Flageolet.
9: Bugle. 10: Rattle. 11: Music box. 12: Metallophone.

1, 4, 6, 7, 9: Music boxes. 2, 5, 8: Roller organs. 3: Gramophone.

68

Franz Liszt conducting one of his oratorios.

70   1: Richard Wagner. 2: Giuseppe Verdi. 3: Jenny Lind. 4: Franz Liszt. 5: Hector Berlioz.

1: Joseph Haydn. 2: George Frederick Handel. 3: Wolfgang Amadeus Mozart. 4: Christoph
Willibald von Gluck. 5: Johann Sebastian Bach. 6: Ludwig van Beethoven.

1: Franz Schubert. 2: Richard Wagner. 3: Robert Schumann. 4: Johannes Brahms. 5: Felix Mendelssohn-Bartholdy. 6: Carl Maria von Weber.

1: Shofar.

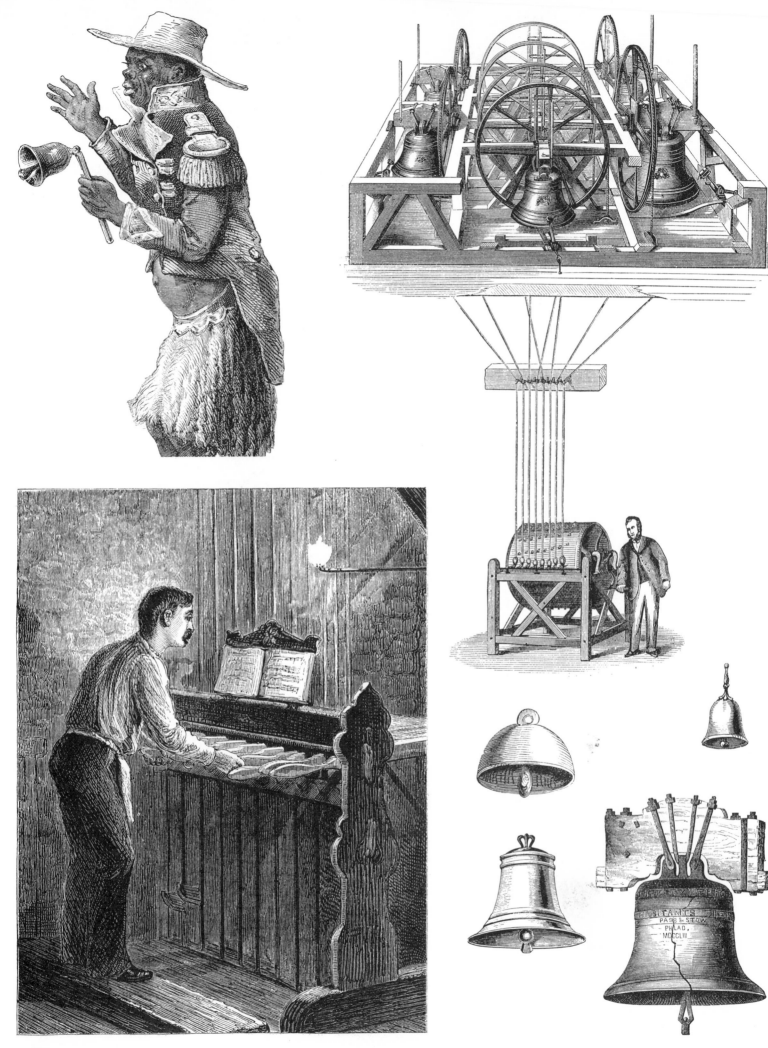

1 & 2: Egyptian harps. 3: Celtic harp.

1: Conch.

1: Egyptian cithara. 2: Sistrum. 3 & 4: Ancient harps. 5: Cymbals. 6: Greek cithara. 7: Psaltery.

81

84

1: Tambourine. 2: Sarangi.

1: Nay.

88

1: Mijwiz. 2: Arghool.

1: Ram's horn. **2**: Simple marimba. **3**: Ivory trumpet.

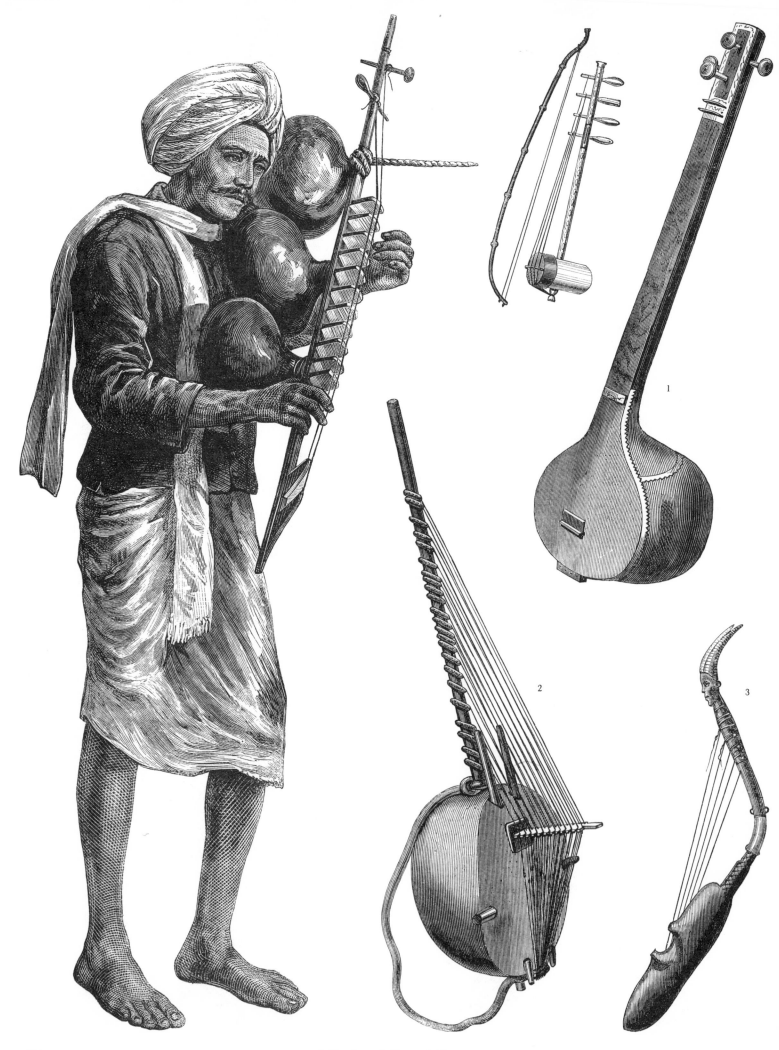

1: Tambura. 2: Kasso. 3: Nanga.

1: Marimba. 2: Kuitra. 3: Tarau.

1: Yüeh-ch'ing. **2**: Small Chinese drum.

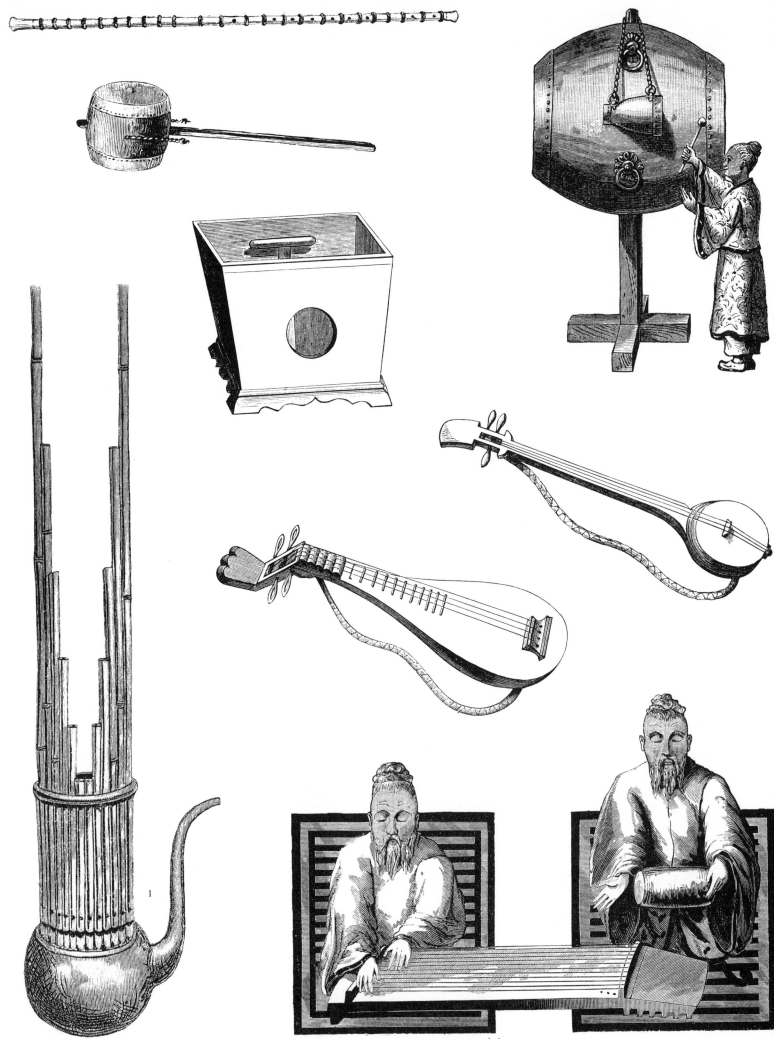

Various Chinese instruments. No. 1 is a type of sheng.

1: Takigoto. 2: Nallari. 3: Hichiriki. 4: Sheng.

99

1: Bells of the Chiriquí Indians. 2–4: Chiriquí whistles.

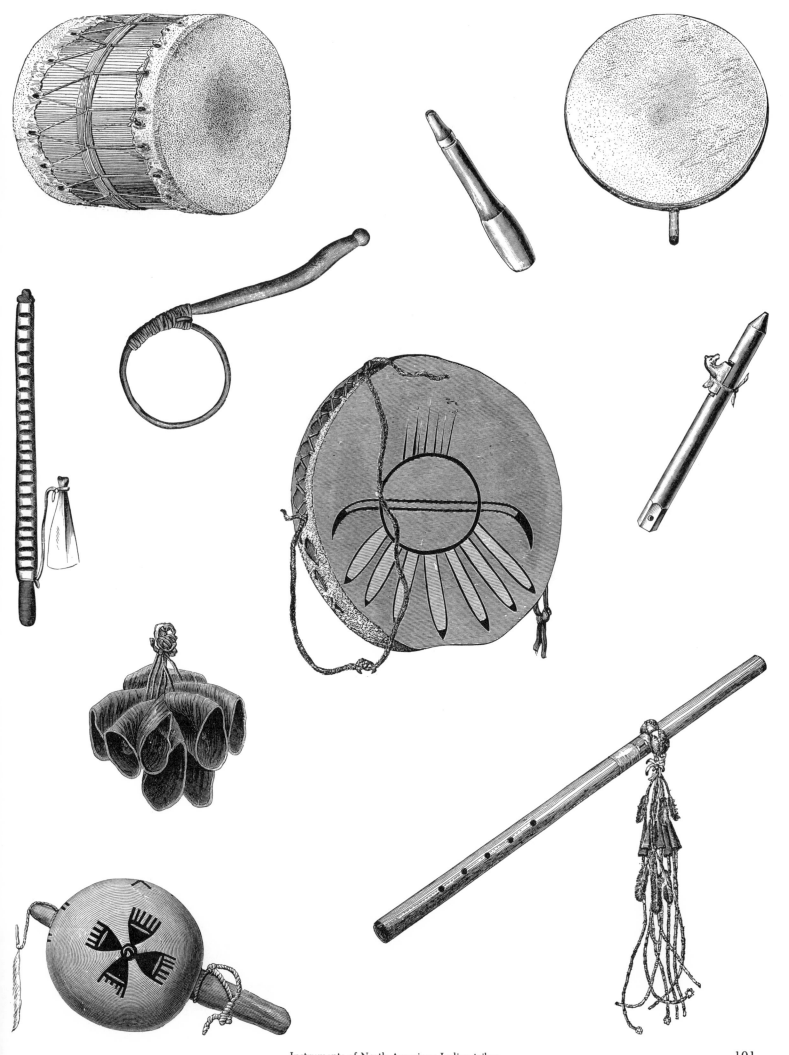

Instruments of North American Indian tribes.

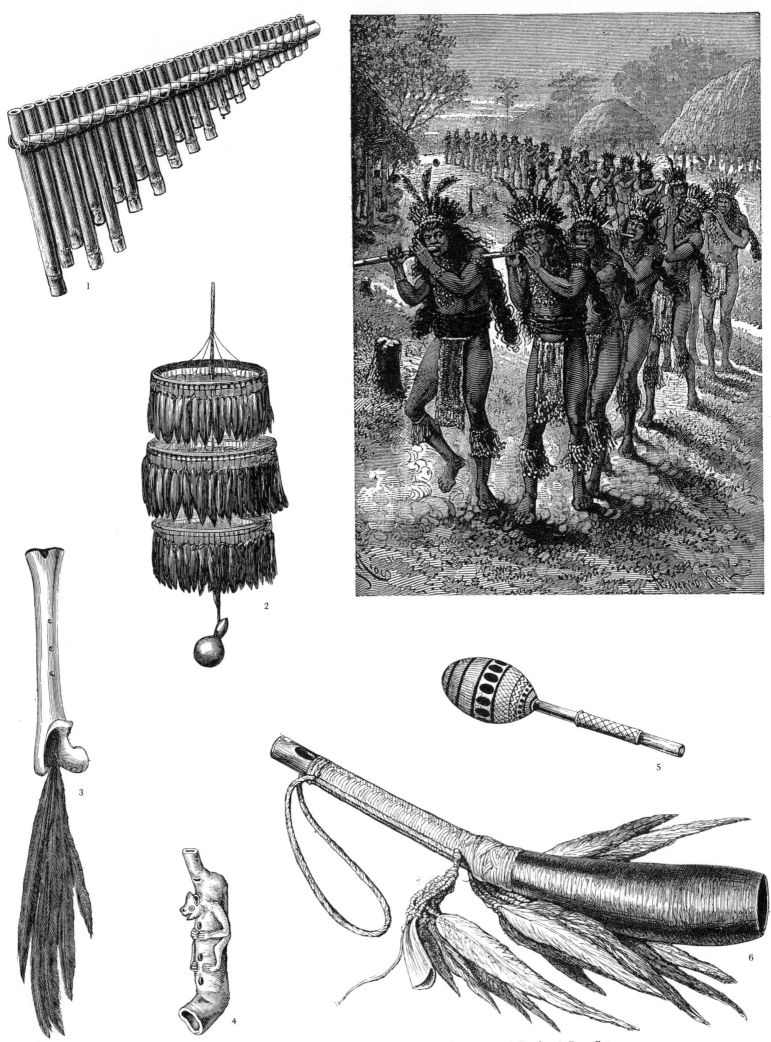

Instruments of Central and South American Indians. 1: Reed pipes. 2 & 5: Rattles. 3: Bone flute.
4: Whistle. 6: War trumpet.

The Dance.

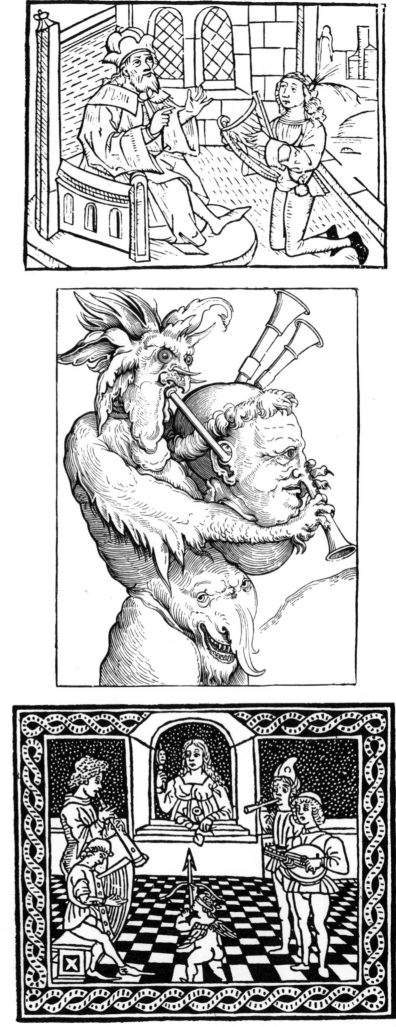

1: Olifant.

1 & 2: Violins.

1: Mountain horn. 2: Recorder. 3: Cittern. 4: Serinette. 5: Machete. 6: Lute. 7: Harp-lute.

1: Spanish guitar. 2: Viola da gamba.

1: Mandore. **2 & 3**: Mandolins. **4**: Archlute. **5**: Lute.

1: Violoncello. 2: Viola da gamba. 3: Violin. 4: Viola d'amore. 5: Violino piccolo.

1 & 2: Oboes. **3 & 4:** Flutes. **5:** Alto recorder. **6:** Pipe. **7 & 8:** Fifes. **9:** Flageolet.

121

1: Tabor. 2: Serpent. 3: Gong. 4: Tromba marina.

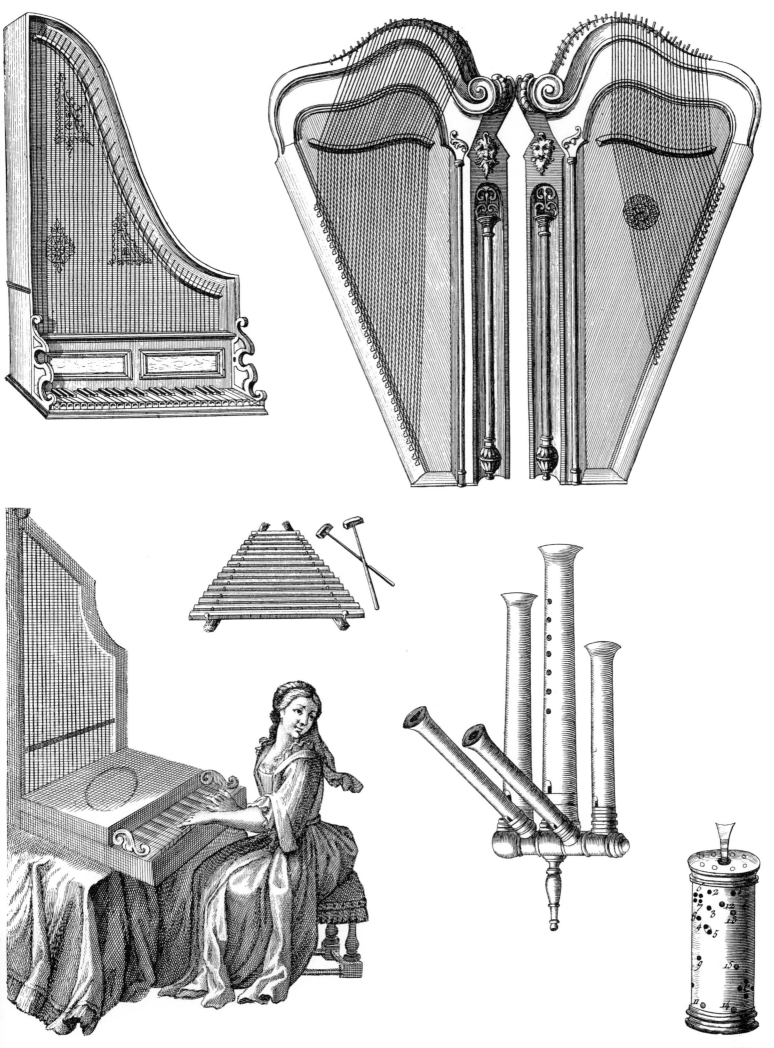

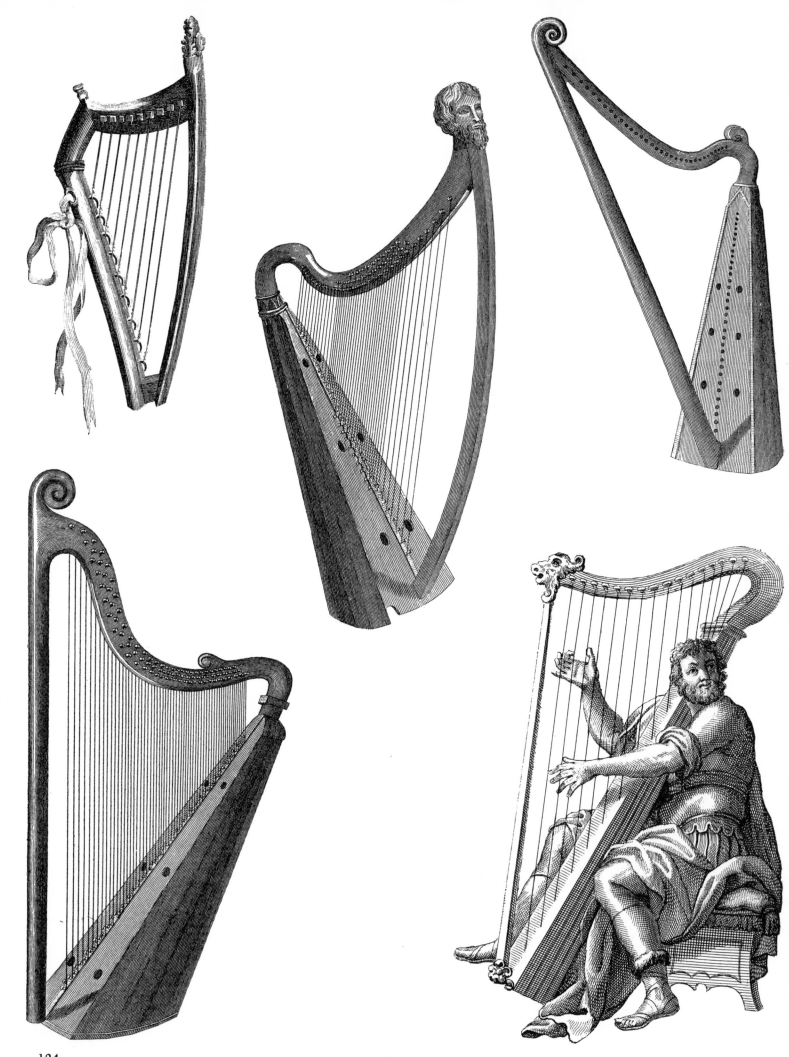

Harps.

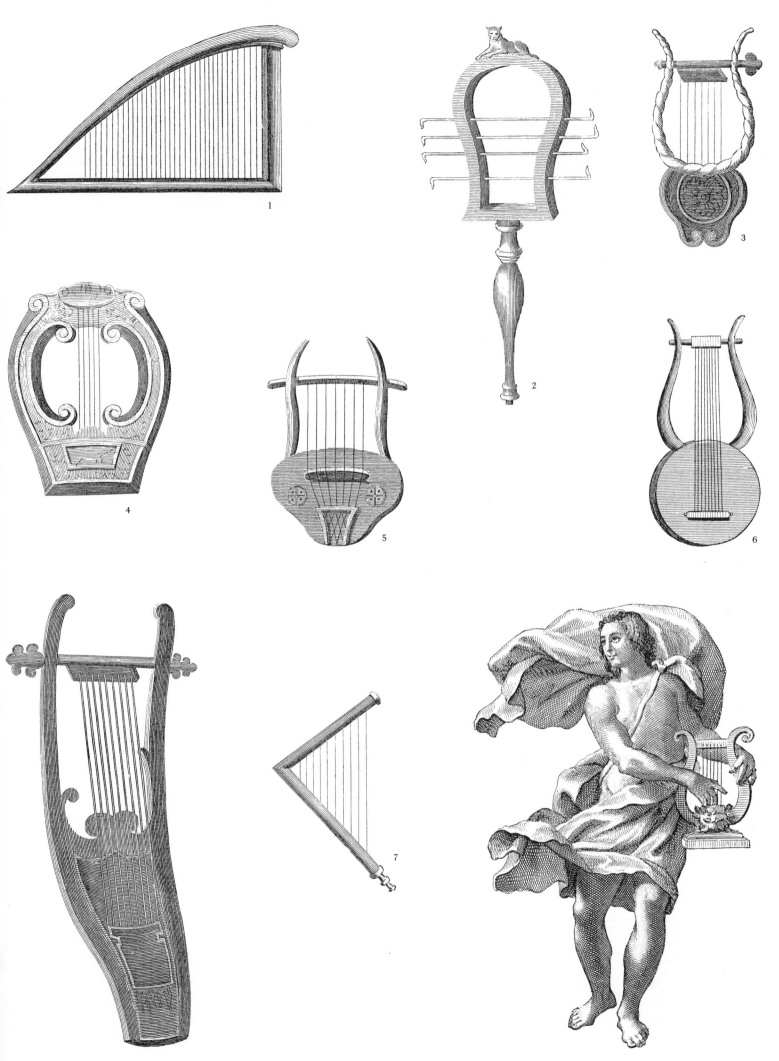

1: Ancient harp. 2: Sistrum. 3–6: Lyres. 7: Trigonium.

126

128

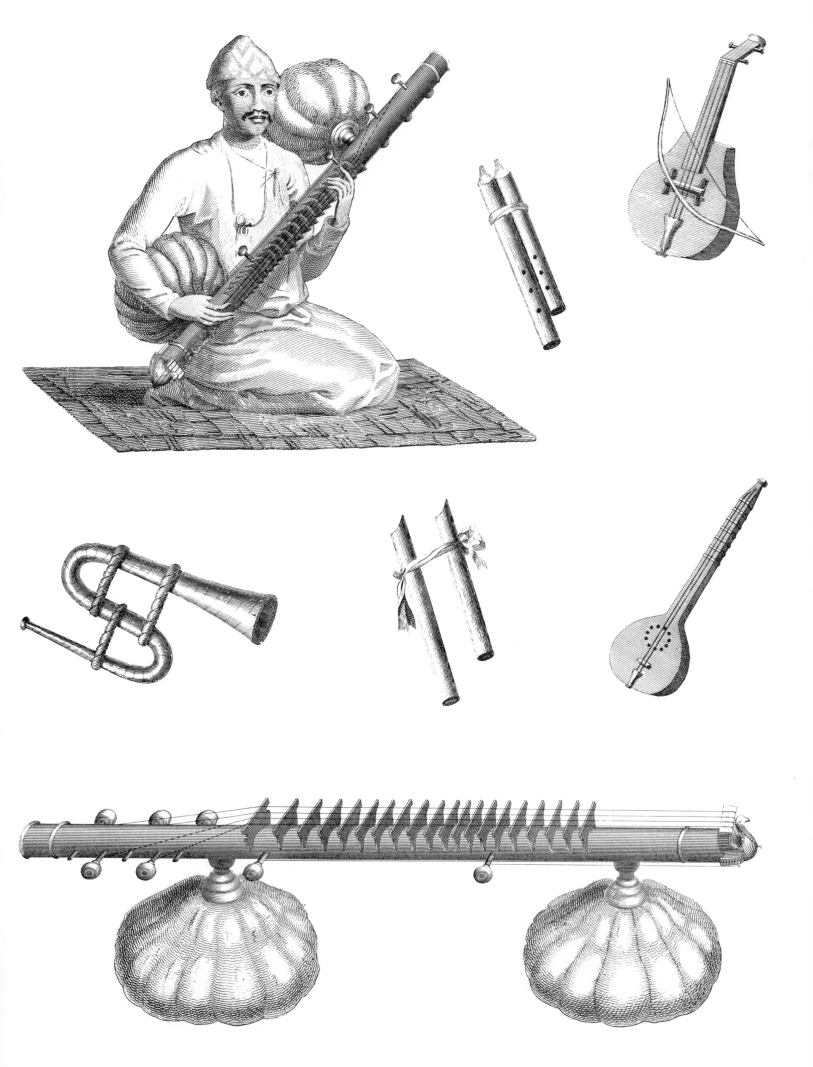

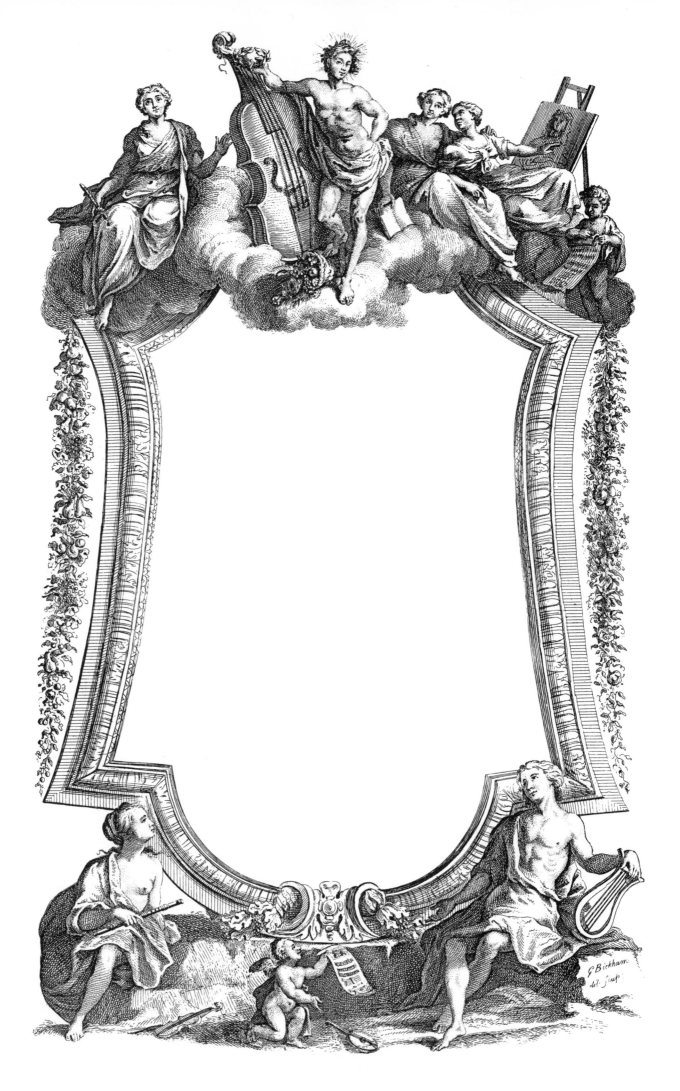

DISCANTVS.
Der newen deudsch
en geistlichen lieder.

136

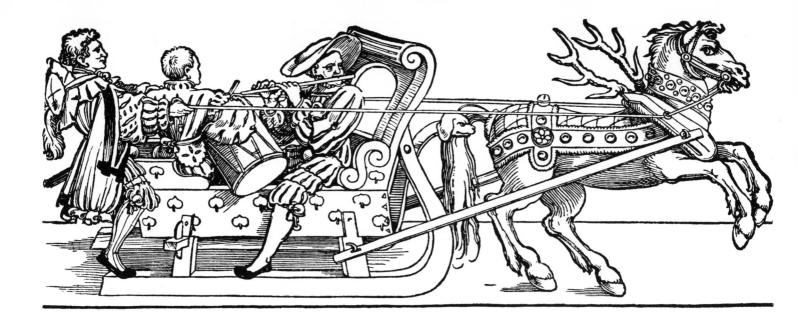

So König Arggus dann entschlieff/
Wie man mit einer Pfeiffen pfeiff:
Wie solt er nicht entschlaffen sein/
Wann er solt hören heut allein

Ein Orgel mit so vilen stimmen/
Die man nicht kan genugsam rühmen/
Von wegen kunst vnd lieblichkeit/
Die also ist fürtrefflich heut/

Das Apollo (ders erstlich lehrt)
Sich müßt vertriechen/wann ers hört/
Wiewol er den Marsiam schund 4
Der erst zwo Pfeiffen zammen bund.

Ein Slehrter schreibt: der Krieg sei hart:
Derhalben auch erfunden ward
Hart Meßing Instrument zur sach/
Welchs noch die Leut vil härter mach/

Ja das die Pferd dahin kan pringen/
Das sie zur schlacht gantz fräudig springe:
Josephus schreibt/ das Moses eben
Hat die Meßin Trommet angeben/

Dargegen schreibet Plinius
Der Tirrhenisch König Priscus
Hab mit seim Volck die auf gebracht/
Im Krieg ward bessers nie erdacht. 8

Mar manche Pfeiff erfand der Pan/
Von dem nichts häßlichs komen kan/
Weil er soll sein der Bauren Gott:
Der hat zusamen auch gerott

Die Rußpfeiff/ Schalmey/ wie man meint/
Die Sackpfeiff sey in auch verfreunt/
Weich man zwar muß lan passieren/
Das sie der Musick Namen füren:

Dann so die Musick ist vmb freud
Erdacht/ vnd vmb ergetzlichkeyt/
So muß man sie nit schlecht verlachen/
Die weil sie auch vil kurtzweil machen. 9

Wiewol Minerve gar miß fällt
Die Pfeif/ weil sie den mund verstelt/
Soll man sich doch nicht ärgern lon/
Dann sie red wie ein Weib dar von:

Vnd vil mehr auf Poeten geben
Die solche Pfeif gar hoch erheben/
Weil sie inn der Natur bestehet
Vnd auch zu allen Spilen gehet.

Die Zwerchpfeif erstlich Midas macht
Nur auß Kran/ beinen ingeschlacht:
Die man darnach macht auß den Roten
Heut kan man sie zum schönsten boren. 5

144

Wann man die Warheit sagen will/
So ist die Geig das ältest Spil/
Welchs Jubal vor der Sündflut fand
Deß sich darnach auch vnterwand

Apollo/ für ein Gott gehalten/
Vnd schreiben doch dabei die Alten
Das im die Geigen geben hab
Mercurius/ für ein Heroldstab/

Die hat trei Styten vberauß
Gspannt vber ein Merschneckenhauß:
Vil Instrument von ir entspringen:
Drum libt man sie vor allen dingk. 2

Die schön Spartanisch Policei/
Wie sie groß Krig fürt mancherlei/
Da hat sie auch gantz wol bedacht/
Die Zinkenhörner auffgepracht:

Das man sie praucht zu Feld im Hör/
Auff das sie machten ghertzter mehr/
Damit zu geben auch ein zeichen
Wa man vom Feind hin solte weichen/

Vnd in was schritten/ gang/ vnd lauf
An Feind solt gahn der gantze Hauf:
Heut aber seinds im Krig abkomen/
Man praucht dafür Trometk Tronk. 7

DAS Harpret ist ein alter fund/
Sein vrsprung aber ist nicht kund:
Doch meinen etlich für gewiß/
Das von der Harpfen es entspriß

Vnd von David sei erstlich gstifft/
Vnd wie solchs bezeügt Joseph Schrifft/
Der schreibt/ das David hab gar vil/
Erfunden newen Seitenspil/

Vnd außgetheilt vnn die Leviten/
Einsonder Instrument ein jeden/
Deren eins soll das Harpret sein:
Bei Frauen ist es sehr gemein: 6

ES Wider beiin selbs eracht/
Das die Quintern fein nach gemacht/
Der Geigen/ wie sich das befind/
Wer irem vrsprung recht nach grünt/

Vnd nur das Instrument besicht:
Ward erstlich nur dahin gericht/
Auff das sie ein anleitung sey
Zur Lauten/ vnd zu allerlei/

Auch das man Lider darzu dicht/
Vnd sing darein ein alt geschicht:
Gleich wie auch thaten vnsere Alten
Drum wöllen wir sie noch erhalten.

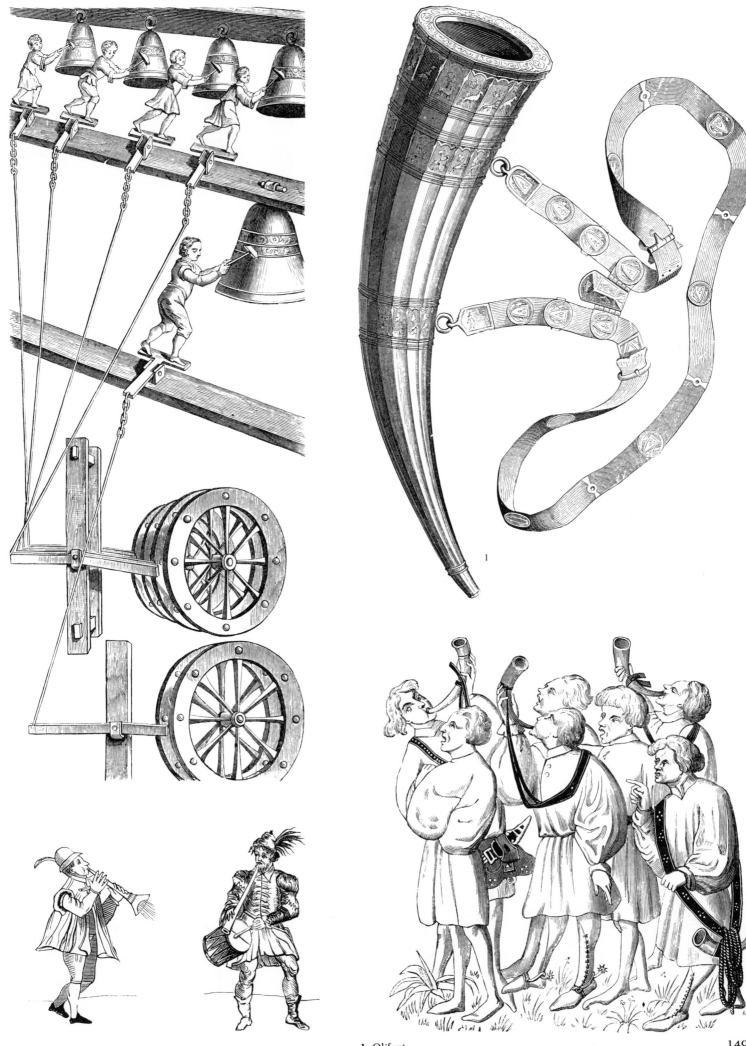

1: Olifant.

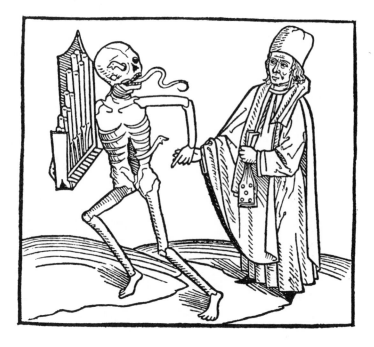

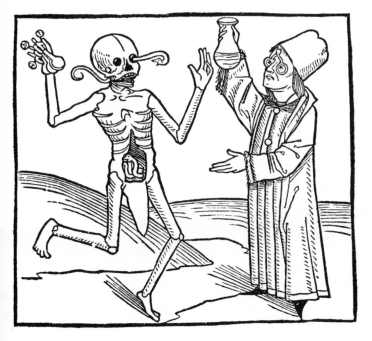

151

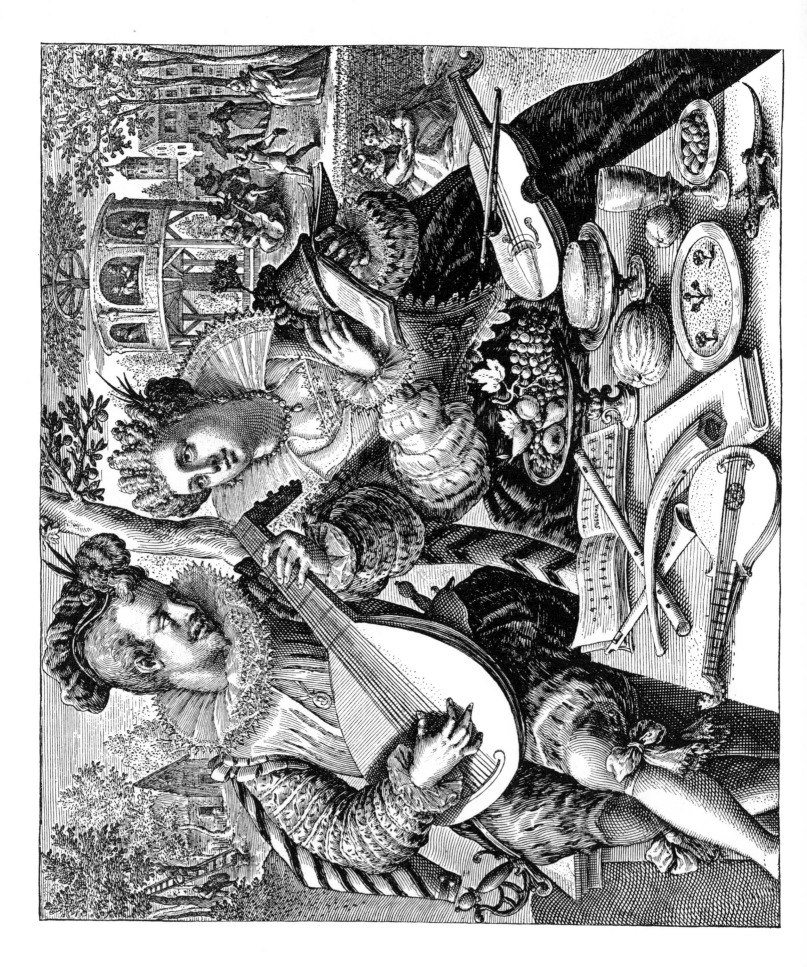

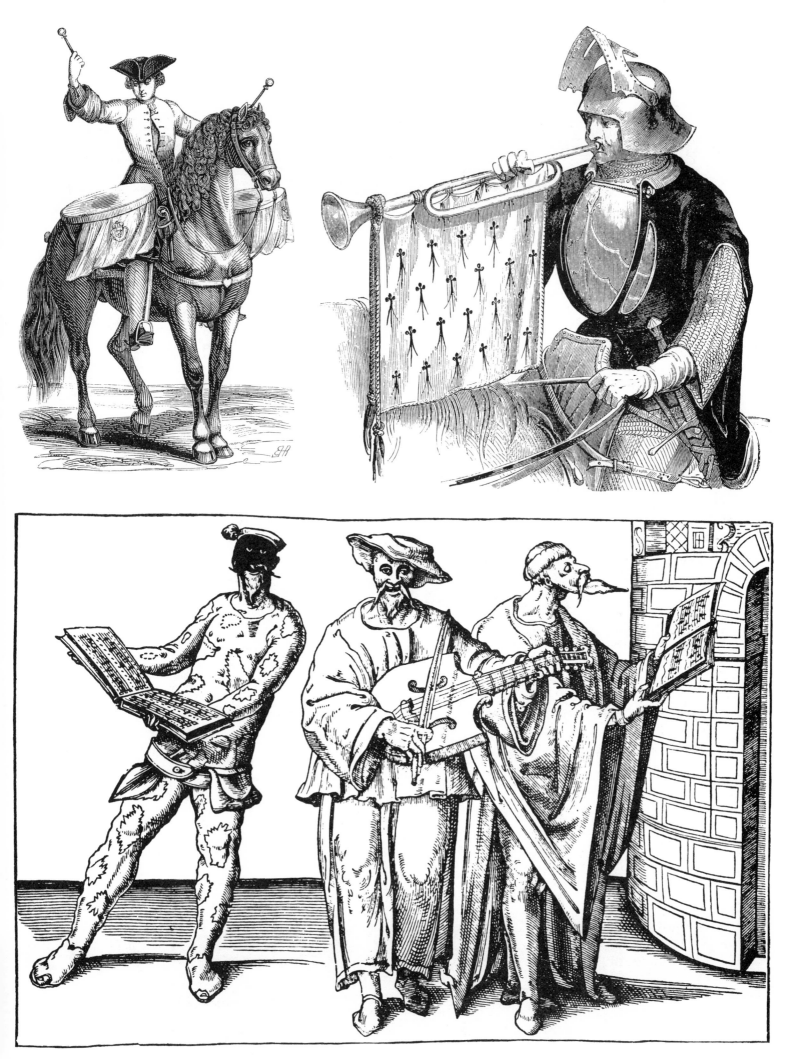

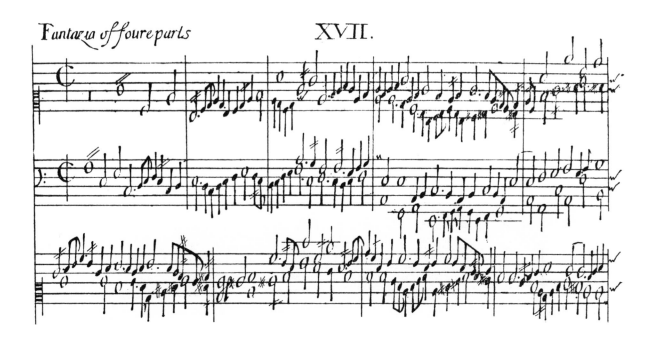